POWER PRAYERS

POWER PRAYERS

For Women To Pray Over The Men
In Their Lives

NINA ELAINE BORUM

Scripture taken from THE JESUS BOOK—The Bible in Worldwide
English. Copyright SOON Educational Publications, Derby DE65 6BN,
UK. Used by permission.

This book is designed to provide accurate and authoritative information
with regard to the subject matter covered. This information is given with the
understanding that neither the author nor Regnum Solum Press is engaged
in rendering legal, professional advice. Since the details of your situation
are fact dependent, you should additionally seek the services of a competent
professional.

Published by Regnum Solum Press, a publishing imprint of Bo Society &
Books 1960 Madison Street, STE J202 | Clarksville, Tennessee USA
www.thebosociety.com

Photo copyright by Erin Grasham
Author Photography by Lindsay Photography

Published in the United States of America

ISBN: 979-8-218-21900-0

Dedication

To my heavenly Father…everything is for your glory. May I always be obedient to your call to glorify you and to produce much fruit. Thank you for using me.

To the men that God gave me:

CJ, for being my big little brother and for still giving me hugs and telling me you love me after every phone call. For always looking out for me and for being you. God has plans for you that your mind cannot even conceive.

Mitchell, for being unapologetically you. You bless me more than you know. You inspire me! Let God lead your life and continue to find your identity in him. You will go places you never imagined!

Clarence, for showing me the beauty of simple faith. For loving momma and for being a constant source of laughter. You are my favorite little old man.

Daddy, for loving the word of God more than anything and for your obedience to the call to go out and make disciples. I love, admire and will always look up to you.

To my mom and sister for constantly supporting my dreams. What would I do without the two of you. Thank you for being my best friends on this earth. I treasure you more than you know. Ladies of Borumnville unite!

Acknowledgments

A heartfelt thanks to all those who ever took a moment to pray for me, support me, mentor me, and most of all believe in what God could do through me. A special thanks to my dear friend and mentor, Margaret Kennell, who is constantly urging me to write, and has always believed that I have a message worth sharing.

I am especially appreciative of: The Salvation Army, the church that has discipled me, challenged me, and supported me. To my Eden Gate small group that constantly attacks me with love.

Table of Contents

POWER IN PURITY

POWER IN OBEDIENCE

POWER IN WISDOM

POWER IN EXHORTATION

POWER IN RESPONSIBILITY

Introduction

The wise prevail through great power and those who
have knowledge muster their strength.

Proverbs 24:5 (WEB)

In a world where it is acceptable to live selfishly and without
holiness, I am thankful for the men who have taken the
narrow road and submitted their lives to the power of God.
As I look at the men in the media who are considered role
models despite their lack of morals and respect for women
and for themselves, I am saddened. When I talk to Christian
male friends and find that their life is more influenced by the
world and their flesh than by the Holy Spirit, I am discour-
aged. When I see men who have been Christian their whole
lives but still don't experience victory in their struggles and
make excuses for themselves, I'm overwhelmed with disbelief.
My heart breaks because of these things and I am reminded
that this is not what God intended for man to be. God created men in his image to show his glory. He created them to
be men of power.

As believers, we have the distinct honor and privilege to
pray for the men in our lives. If we are honest, sometimes we
don't know how to pray or grow weary of doing so. This book

will guide you in praying specifically for the men in your life for the next thirty days. Instead of kneeling and begging, I am challenging you to stand in confidence before the throne and release P.O.W.E.R. in the lives of the men around you.

Jesus Christ has already given us the authority to tear down strongholds, bring healing, and deliverance to the men in our lives. We often forget this and spend time asking God to do something that he has already given us the authority to do in Jesus's name.

Exercise your authority from Christ on behalf of the men that God has placed on your heart. Release Purity, Obedience, Wisdom, Exhortation, and Responsibility in their lives today; and praise God for the transformation that will take place in God's perfect timing.

For the next thirty days, you are challenged to pray specifically for the men in your life. Each day has a brief but powerful prayer. These prayers are not magical formulas. They are blessings that God has already promised his children. You can put your trust in the God that is always faithful to his word and always hears the prayers of the righteous. Let the Holy Spirit guide you in the next thirty days during your prayer time and be open to fasting if the Spirit lays it on your heart.

Have faith as you pray that God is hearing you and answering you. Cast away any feelings of doubt that come to your mind as you pray. Say these prayers with authority because you have the power of the Holy Spirit inside of you. Lastly, say these prayers confidently because they are full of truth. These prayers are crafted directly from the scripture, so we know that these things are within the will of God.

I would recommend saying these prayers out loud and using the specific name of the person you are praying for. There is much power in spoken word. As you pray these prayers out loud, you will in turn increase your faith because faith comes by hearing. The italicized prayer chant will repeat daily. Try to memorize this portion of the prayer so that you can begin to pray it naturally without this prayer guide.

Man of POWER

To this day I have never met a man like him. You only have to encounter him for a moment to know that he is special. The power of God is undeniable in him. His love for God is unquestionable and his faithfulness to the word is unwavering.

In college, my favorite part of Sunday was hearing him preach. He is a good speaker but that's not why I enjoy his messages so much. There are plenty good speakers out there but not all have the power of God flowing like electricity through them. Major Al Smith does. He used to jokingly say that I was dynamite for Jesus, but it is really him that is explosive for Jesus. I wanted to be like him, still do.

His devotion towards holiness is undivided and pure. His obedience in times of trial are inspiring. Wisdom permeates his life. He is always ready to speak the truth in love and he takes his responsibility to spread the gospel seriously.

He is a man of P.O.W.E.R. There must have been people in his life that prayed for him relentlessly. I'm so glad they did. Because of him, I know it's possible for men of God to rise above mediocrity and be men of P.O.W.E.R. Anything is possible when we pray and that is why I wrote this prayer guide.

What is Prayer?

"What the church needs today is not more machinery… not new organizations or more and novel methods, but men whom the Holy ghost can use, men of prayer, men mighty in prayer. The Holy ghost does not flow through methods, but through men. He does not come on machinery, but on men. He does not anoint plans, but men, men of prayer".[1]

"Now I lay me down to sleep, I pray to the Lord, my soul to keep, if I should die before I wake, I pray to the Lord my soul to take, if I should live for other days, I pray to the Lord to guide my ways…". What was this little poem that I recited each night before bed? Was it something to comfort me or something that connected me to the creator?

Maybe it was both. Whichever it was, mothers around the world have made this nighttime prayer a ritual for their sons and daughters. As a child, I don't know how intelligently I would have articulated the definition of prayer but I knew one thing: I couldn't go to sleep until I prayed.

Many of us are taught that prayer is simply talking to God. But let us assume for a brief moment that we know nothing of prayer. If we were discovering prayer for the first time what would the scriptures say about the word prayer? In Genesis 20:7, God comes to Abimelech in a dream and gives him the following instructions concerning Abraham and Sarah. Abimelech had taken Sarah not realizing she was married to Abraham because Abraham lied about his marriage in order to spare his life:

> "Now therefore, restore the man's wife. For he is a prophet, and he will pray for you, and you will live. If you don't restore her, know for sure that you will die, you, and all who are yours."

In Genesis 20:17 we see the results of Abraham's prayer. Abraham prayed to God. God healed Abimelech, and his wife, and his female servants, and they bore children. The Hebrew word that we translate as pray in this particular scriptural context means to pass judgment by making things level or even.

The following is an excerpt from Gesenius' Hebrew-Chaldee Lexicon to the Old Testament on the word "pray" in Genesis 20:7

פָּלַל Pray

> ...the meaning of judging, which is supposed to be derived from that of cutting, deciding,...the primary power of the root to be that of rolling, revolving, *wallen, rollen*...hence to make even by rolling, *to level* with a roller...whence to lay even (a cause), to arbitrate...the sense of making even.[2]

Let's look at the New Testament and find early mentions of prayer. In the New Testament, Jesus Christ is the first to mention prayer. In the book of Matthew Jesus asks his disciples to pray for their enemies. According to the Greek-English Lexicon, the word that we translate as prayer in this context means:

> To speak to or to make requests of God—'to speak to God, to ask God for.'[3]

The Hebrew and Greek meanings of prayer seem different but when put together the meaning of prayer becomes to speak to God in such a way that things are made right. Jesus came to make things right by revealing to us a life that displayed the kingdom of God. How did Jesus live out the kingdom of God? He did this by being obedient to God's will in every area of his life. God's will and his kingdom are peace, love, victory, grace and justice, mercy, hope, etc. Jesus taught his disciples to pray "Your kingdom come, Your will be done". The reign of God is tangible when his will is done in our lives and in the world. Prayer is how we release the kingdom (reign) of God in our lives and in the lives of others. Prayers to make things right (to bring down his kingdom) are always answered because it is God's will.

What a powerful gift and privilege that God has given us. No wonder our mothers found it necessary to instill the discipline of prayer in us. No wonder we could not sleep until this precious work was done.

The Praying Woman

"We talk about how our grandmother and our mothers prayed, how they stayed on their knees until situations changed. We are famous for remembering our grandmothers' prayers, but we are lacking in mimicking them...There is more power when you fall on your face in prayer than in the most powerful atomic missile...."[4]

Often times when we are struggling in prayer we look to Bible stories to encourage us. We remember the persistent widow, the desperate Hagar, the willing Mary and more. The prayers of these women brought about miracles, released blessings, and brought about justice.

As women, we do have some natural advantages in prayers. We are intuitive; we remember details, we are passionate, persistent and good listeners. Though these characteristics help in prayer the active ingredient to old saint's answered prayer was faith.

God showed these saints favor in prayer. If we desire to have favor in our prayers we should take note of the faith of the following women.

The story of the Canannite's woman prayer shows faith even after Jesus initially ignores her prayer and then tells her no twice.

Jesus went out from there, and withdrew into the region of Tyre and Sidon. Behold, a Canaanite woman came out from those borders, and cried, saying, "Have mercy on me, Lord, you son of David! My daughter is severely possessed by a demon!"

But he answered her not a word.

His disciples came and begged him, saying, "Send her away; for she cries after us."

But he answered, "I wasn't sent to anyone but the lost sheep of the house of Israel."

But she came and worshiped him, saying, "Lord, help me."

But he answered, "It is not appropriate to take the children's bread and throw it to the dogs."

But she said, "Yes, Lord, but even the dogs eat the crumbs which fall from their masters' table."

Then Jesus answered her, "Woman, great is your faith! Be it done to you even as you desire." And her daughter was healed from that hour.

Matthew 15:21-28 (WEB)

The story of Anna's prayer life is short but powerful. What would your prayer life look like if you had lost your husband and never remarried? Her example of prayer teaches us to have faith despite our circumstances and feelings.

There was one Anna, a prophetess, the daughter of Phanuel, of the tribe of Asher (she was of a great age, having lived with a husband seven years from her virginity, and she had been a widow for about eighty-four years), who didn't depart from the temple, worshiping with fastings and petitions night and day. Coming up at that very hour, she gave thanks to the

Lord, and spoke of him to all those who were looking for redemption in Jerusalem.

Luke 2:36-38 (WEB)

Perhaps, the example of Hannah's prayer is one that we can all relate to. We have all felt bitter and deeply wounded. In moments like these, we are called to pray and believe that God will turn our bitterness to joy.

So Hannah rose up after they had finished eating and drinking in Shiloh. Now Eli the priest was sitting on his seat by the doorpost of Yahweh's temple. She was in bitterness of soul, and prayed to Yahweh, weeping bitterly. She vowed a vow, and said, "Yahweh of Armies, if you will indeed look at the affliction of your servant, and remember me, and not forget your servant, but will give to your servant a boy, then I will give him to Yahweh all the days of his life, and no razor shall come on his head."

As she continued praying before Yahweh, Eli saw her mouth. Now Hannah spoke in her heart. Only her lips moved, but her voice was not heard. Therefore Eli thought she was drunk. Eli said to her, "How long will you be drunk? Get rid of your wine!"

Hannah answered, "No, my lord, I am a woman of a sorrowful spirit. I have not been drinking wine or strong drink, but I poured out my soul before Yahweh. Don't consider your servant a wicked woman; for I have been speaking out of the abundance of my complaint and my provocation." Then Eli answered, "Go in peace; and may the God of Israel grant your petition that you have asked of him."

She said, "Let your servant find favor in your sight." So the woman went her way, and ate; and her facial expression wasn't sad any more.

1 Samuel 1:9-18 (WEB)

Last but not least, one the most bittersweet prayers in the Bible was not uttered by a woman but by our Savior. Jesus teaches us to be prepared for God to answer our prayers with a firm no if it does not align with his will. Jesus prays this request twice to no avail.

Then Jesus came with them to a place called Gethsemane, and said to his disciples, "Sit here, while I go there and pray." He took with him Peter and the two sons of Zebedee, and began to be sorrowful and severely troubled. Then he said to them, "My soul is exceedingly sorrowful, even to death. Stay here, and watch with me." He went forward a little, fell on his face, and prayed, saying, "My Father, if it is possible, let this cup pass away from me; nevertheless, not what I desire, but what you desire…Again, a second time he went away, and prayed, saying, "My Father, if this cup can't pass away from me unless I drink it, your desire be done."

Matthew 26:36-39, 42

Calling on the Lord to bring about his kingdom and will is no small matter. Entering into such a conversation involves a faith that takes times to develop and a trust that stands even after God says no. Are you ready to pray with the same humility, courage, determination and persistence as the saints?

Before You Pray: Prayer Checklist

☐ Be Right With God

Beloved, if our hearts don't condemn us, we have boldness toward God; and whatever we ask, we receive from him, because we keep his commandments and do the things that are pleasing in his sight.

1 John 3:21–22 (WEB)

☐ Be Humble

Abraham answered, See now, I have taken it on myself to speak to the Lord, although I am dust and ashes.

Genesis 18:27 (WEB)

☐ Be Expectant

Yahweh, in the morning you shall hear my voice. In the morning I will lay my requests before you, and will watch expectantly.

Psalm 5:3 (WEB)

☐ Be Bold

This is the boldness which we have toward him, that, if we ask anything according to his will, he listens to us. And if we know that he listens to us, whatever we ask, we know that we have the petitions which we have asked of him.

1 John 5:14–15 (WEB)

☐ Have Faith

Jesus answered them, "Most certainly I tell you, if you have faith, and don't doubt, you will not only do what was done to the fig tree, but even if you told this mountain, be taken up and cast into the sea, it would be done. All things, whatever you ask in prayer, believing, you will receive."

Matthew 21:21–22 (WEB)

☐ Be Persistent

He also spoke a parable to them that they must always pray, and not give up, saying, "There was a judge in a certain city who didn't fear God, and didn't respect man. A widow was in that city, and she often came to him, saying, Defend me from my adversary! He wouldn't for a while, but afterward he said to himself, Though I neither fear God, nor respect man, yet because this widow bothers me, I will defend her, or else she will wear me out by her continual coming. The Lord said, "Listen to what the unrighteous judge says. Won't God avenge his chosen ones, who are crying out to him day and night, and yet he exercises patience with them? I tell you that he will avenge them quickly. Nevertheless, when the Son of Man comes, will he find faith on the earth?

Luke 18:1–8 (WEB)

☐ Don't Worry

In nothing be anxious, but in everything, by prayer and petition with thanksgiving, let your requests be made known to God. And the peace of God, which surpasses all understanding, will guard your hearts and your thoughts in Christ Jesus.

Philippians 4:6–7 (WEB)

☐ Have Authority

He called the twelve together, and gave them power and authority over all demons, and to cure diseases. He sent them out to preach God's Kingdom and to heal the sick.

Luke 9:1–2 (WEB)

☐ Count On The Impossible

These signs will accompany those who believe: in my name they will cast out demons; they will speak with new languages; they will take up serpents; and if they drink any deadly thing, it will in no way hurt them; they will lay hands on the sick, and they will recover.

Mark 16:17–18 (WEB)

Setting the Mood

When was the last time you experienced quiet? Every day we are bombarded by noise. In the morning you are gently awakened by your spouse moving around the room, you hear the shower going, you hear the pitter patter of little feet, you hear the A/C running, the morning news, the radio in the car, co-workers talking, phones ringing, and of course the hundreds of random thoughts that run through your head.

When we pray we must remember that we are entering the spiritual realm. We are defying the laws of the physical world and connecting with the Divine. We should go into prayer with the attitude of reverence, respect and adoration. We should prepare our hearts and minds for this heavenly communication and not go into it lightly and hurriedly.

Prayer Space: The space should be uncluttered so that you are not distracted. If you like connecting with God through photos, feel free to put up inspirational photos or quotes. The space should be quiet. Don't let the silence scare you but use it as a time to listen to the Lord's voice.

Prayer Place: Your living room is a dedicated place for entertaining family and friends, your kitchen is dedicated for family meals, your bedroom is dedicated for intimate time with your spouse, why not have a space dedicated for intentional time with the Lord. A corner in a living room, your porch, maybe the shower, window seat or kitchen table. Prayer does not have to happen only in this place, however, it is beneficial to dedicate a space in your home to connect with God.

Prayer Time: The spiritual giants in my life have all adopted morning prayer times in addition to evening prayer times. If you are not a morning person, your "morning" starts when you awake. The point is that it is to your benefit to begin and end your day, whatever time that may be, with prayer. Praying without ceasing means that we should be consistently connected to the spirit realm, this is called communing with God.

Prayer Items: What objects do you use in prayer? Willow tree angels and candles decorate my personal prayer space.

Perhaps you have a favorite cross, a soft pillow to kneel on, your grandmother's quilt blanket to sit on or music that leads your time of praise. Use these items to enhance your prayer space and to designate it as a special space.

Prayer and Fasting Challenge

When Jesus saw that a multitude came running together, he rebuked the unclean spirit, saying to him, "You mute and deaf spirit, I command you, come out of him, and never enter him again!"

Having cried out, and convulsed greatly, it came out of him. The boy became like one dead; so much that most of them said, "He is dead." But Jesus took him by the hand, and raised him up; and he arose.

When he had come into the house, his disciples asked him privately, "Why couldn't we cast it out?" He said to them, "This kind can come out by nothing, except by prayer and fasting."

Mark 9:25–29 (WEB)

I dare you to pray consistently for the next 30 days for the men in your life. If we are honest, sometimes our prayer life is haphazard and spur of the moment. Challenge yourself to be disciplined this month concerning praying for the specific men in your life.

Life can be busy and the last thing most people want to do is add on to their to do list. The scripted prayers in this book are brief and easy to memorize so that you can meditate on them throughout the day.

Fasting combined with faithful prayer can cast out demons. Jesus alludes to this when he tells disciples that some things only come out through prayer and fasting. A great way to jumpstart your 30 days of intentional prayer is with a fast. Fasting has been known to bring about miraculous results in the lives of saints.

- ❏ Esther fasted to save her people. (Esther 4:16)
- ❏ Jesus fasted and overcame the temptation of Satan (Luke 4:1-12)
- ❏ Cornelius fasted and was visited by a messenger of God (Acts 10:30-33)
- ❏ Saul fasts for 3 days and is prepared for earth shattering ministry. (Acts 9:9)
- ❏ Moses fasted and wrote the Ten Commandments. (Exodus 34:28)

I wonder what God could do through you if in faith and trust you fasted the next thirty days? The biblical example of fasting is to go without food or certain types of food. Both the Greek and Hebrew word for fast deal with abstaining specifically from food. During the season of Lent, many people will boast to their church, their friends and on their social medial pages about what they are giving up. But this is not the example of fasting that the Bible has set for us.

Moreover when you fast, don't be like the hypocrites, with sad faces. For they disfigure their faces, that they may be seen by men to be fasting. Most certainly I tell you, they have received their reward. But you, when you fast, anoint your head, and wash your face; so that you are not seen by men to be fasting, but by your Father who is in secret, and your Father, who sees in secret, will reward you.

Boasting about fasting chocolate, carbonated beverages or meats and secretly desiring to lose weight is not what the Lord desires from our fasting. Your fasting should bring you to a point of humility and spiritual growth. Keeping your fast between you and the Lord will yield a reward that is eternal which is more than a few temporary pounds.

Let the Holy Spirit lead you in how to fast as you prepare for the next 30 days. Remember that God is pleased when our fasting comes with a pure heart. Isaiah 58:3-9 speaks on this:

Why have we fasted,' say they, 'and you don't see?
Why have we afflicted our soul, and you don't notice?'
"Behold, in the day of your fast you find pleasure,
and oppress all your laborers.
Behold, you fast for strife and contention,
and to strike with the fist of wickedness.
You don't fast today so as to make your voice to be heard
on high.
Is this the fast that I have chosen?
A day for a man to humble his soul?
Is it to bow down his head like a reed,
and to spread sackcloth and ashes under himself?
Will you call this a fast,
and an acceptable day to Yahweh?
"Isn't this the fast that I have chosen:
to release the bonds of wickedness,
to undo the straps of the yoke,
to let the oppressed go free,
and that you break every yoke?

Isn't it to distribute your bread to the hungry,
and that you bring the poor who are cast out to your house?
When you see the naked,
that you cover him;
and that you not hide yourself from your own flesh?
Then your light will break out as the morning,
and your healing will appear quickly;
then your righteousness shall go before you;
and Yahweh's glory will be your rear guard.
Then you will call, and Yahweh will answer;
you will cry for help, and he will say, 'Here I am.'

There are a variety of fasts found in the scriptures. God does not call everyone to an absolute fast (no food or water) so be wise. Partial fasts are recommended for longer periods of time because you abstain from specific foods and not food altogether. A corporate fast can be beneficial as it keeps you encouraged and has built in accountability. Please consult your doctor before entering into fasting.

Battle List

List the names of the men that you are going to spiritual battle for. Indicate the date you began this prayer challenge on their behalf. In the journal pages that follow be sure to add any praise reports concerning these men.

Name	Date	Special Notes
Example: Johnny	*12/23/2013*	*Deliverance from depression*

Nina Elaine Borum

Name	Date	Special Notes

POWER IN PURITY

Blessed are the pure in heart for they
shall see God.

Matthew 5:8 (WEB)

Pure Devotion

A pure devotion for God can be rare among Christians. We are so influenced by the world that we don't even realize that our walk with God is polluted. Psalm 119 gives us a roadmap for purity. If you want to check and see if your walk with God is pure, consider these questions:

Have you lived according to God's word? Not what makes sense, not your opinions, not what feels right, not what your heart says, or what the world says is right.

How have you sought the Lord? By a quick prayer on a Sunday morning, by seeking him only when you need his advice, or have you done it with your whole heart?

Have you ever made the decision not to sin because you remember God's truth? Or do you justify your actions and search for scriptures that will support your behavior?

Have you allowed the Holy Spirit to teach you the ways of God or do you just follow the popular cause.

What have you declared with your lips? Think about the things you say to yourself and others throughout the day.

Do you truly delight in God's statutes or do you see them as outdated and irrelevant when it's a statute that you don't personally agree with.

Did you find these questions convicting? Did you find yourself justifying your answers?

It is easy to slowly but surely have an impure walk with God. This Psalm encourages us to get back on the right path. The grace of God is with those who are seeking to follow him in purity.

This week as you pray for the men in your life, remember how easy it is to fall off the path and pray all the more for them.

DAY 1

Father, I thank you today that _____ is keeping his way pure. I release a hunger for your word into his heart that he may desire to live according to it. May he seek you with every fiber of his being and thirst for you daily. I rebuke any plans of Satan that would deceive him to stray from your commands. Hide your word in his heart that he may not sin against you. Lord, be slow to anger concerning any idols in his life. Convict him with the areas of his life that he has broken his covenant with you. Open his eyes to see the things, people, opinions, ideas, organizations, etc. that he has put before you. May he be pure in his covenant with you.

How can a young man keep his way pure? By living according to your word. With my whole heart, I have sought you. Don't let me wander from your commandments. I have hidden your word in my heart that I might not sin against you. Blessed are you, Yahweh. Teach me your statutes. With my lips, I have declared all the ordinances of your mouth.

Psalms 119:9–13 (web)

Let Samaria throw out his calf idol! My anger burns against them! How long will it be until they are capable of purity?

Hosea 8:5 (web)

JOURNAL

_____

_____

_____

_____

_____

_____

_____

_____

_____

_____

_____

_____

_____

_____

_____

_____

_____

_____

_____

_____

_____

_____

_____

_____

_____

_____

_____

DAY 2

Father, today I lift up _____ to your throne. May his heart be overwhelmed by the power of your sacred love. Reveal to him how high, how deep, and how wide your love is for him. Grant him the gift of discernment and wisdom, that he will be confident of your will. Clothe him in purity so that he would be blameless in your sight. Replace his lifeless deeds with fruits of righteousness that can come only from you. Lead him to repentance and fill his mouth with praise and his countenance with your glory. Lord, make him an example to other men around him as his words and actions and beliefs are grounded in purity. May his trust be always in you and your ways.

This I pray, that your love may abound yet more and more in knowledge and all discernment; so that you may approve the things that are excellent; that you may be sincere and without offense to the day of Christ; being filled with the fruits of righteousness, which are through Jesus Christ, to the glory and praise of God.

Philippians 1:9–11 (WEB)

This saying is faithful and worthy of all acceptance. For to this end we both labor and suffer reproach, because we have set our trust in the living God, who is the Savior of all men, especially of those who believe. Command and teach these things. Let no man despise your youth; but be an example to those who believe, in word, in your way of life, in love, in spirit, in faith, and in purity.

1 Timothy: 4:9-12 (WEB)

JOURNAL

_____
_____
_____
_____
_____
_____
_____
_____
_____
_____
_____
_____
_____
_____
_____
_____
_____
_____
_____
_____
_____
_____
_____
_____
_____

DAY 3

Lord, forgive _____ for the times he has chosen his own way instead of yours. Be merciful to him and those influenced by any of his wrongdoings. Teach him a new way of thinking so that he would be led by the mind of Christ and not by the emotions of his heart. Renew a steadfast spirit within him. Bless him with your continued presence and make your Spirit move in him. Remind him today of the true joy found only in your salvation. Sustain him and grant him the desire to surrender his will daily to you. Make his heart ready to stand before you. Keep him from falling into lies of the world and keep his hands clean from wickedness. Bless him with righteousness and salvation as he seeks you with his whole heart.

Hide your face from my sins, and blot out all of my iniquities. Create in me a clean heart, O God. Renew a right spirit within me. Don't throw me from your presence and don't take your holy Spirit from me. Restore to me the joy of your salvation. Uphold me with a willing spirit.

Psalm 51:9–12 (web)

Who may ascend to Yahweh's hill? Who may stand in his holy place? He who has clean hands and a pure heart; who has not lifted up his soul to falsehood, and has not sworn deceitfully. He shall receive a blessing from Yahweh, righteousness from the God of his salvation. This is the generation of those who seek Him, who seek your face—even Jacob. Selah.

Psalm 24:3-6 (web)

JOURNAL

_____

_____

_____

_____

_____

_____

_____

_____

_____

_____

_____

_____

_____

_____

_____

_____

_____

_____

_____

_____

_____

DAY 4

Father, I thank you for granting _____
the peace of Christ Jesus that will guard his heart and
mind today and forever. I pray that every negative
thought today would be destroyed by thoughts of truth
and nobility. Open his mind to see life through a lens
of righteousness, loveliness, and most of all purity. Sur-
round him today with things that are praiseworthy and
excellent. Inspire him consistently through messages of
truth, the reading of your word and accountability from
other men who follow you closely. Cleanse his mind,
his heart and renew his spirit. Wash him from any hint
of impurity. Reveal to him ways in which he has defiled
his flesh and lead him to repentance. Perfect his holiness
in your time.

And the peace of God, which surpasses all understanding,
will guard your hearts and your thoughts in Christ Jesus.
Finally, brothers, whatever things are true, whatever things
are honorable, whatever things are just, whatever things are
pure, whatever things are lovely, whatever things are of good
report; if there is any virtue, and if there is any praise, think
about these things. The things which you learned, received,
heard, and saw in me: do these things, and the God of peace
will be with you.

Philippians 4:7–9 (WEB)

Having therefore these promises, beloved, let us cleanse ourselves from all defilement of flesh and spirit, perfecting holiness in the fear of God.

2 Corinthians 7:1 (WEB)

JOURNAL

_____

_____

_____

_____

_____

_____

_____

_____

_____

_____

_____

_____

_____

_____

_____

_____

_____

_____

_____

_____

_____

_____

_____

_____

_____

_____

DAY 5

May _____ put his trust in your word as it refreshes his soul. Make your law perfect in his sight. I pray that he would grow to know you as faithful and in response live faithfully to you. Send joy to overflow his heart as he learns that your ways are right. Make the light of your commands radiate through his eyes and smile. Give him a lasting fear of you that makes him pure. May he find satisfaction in your ways alone. Lord, make him like you. You are light and there is no spot of darkness in you, may you cleanse him from all spots of darkness. May he have pure fellowship with you as he sincerely confesses his sin and is humble enough to repent from his mindset and ways. Remind him that you are faithful to forgive so that he does not carry guilt. If he does not find that he needs to repent of sin in his life, firmly remind him that he is a liar and has no fellowship with you until he is humbled in heart.

Yahweh's law is perfect, restoring the soul. Yahweh's testimony is sure, making wise the simple. Yahweh's precepts are right, rejoicing the heart. Yahweh's commandment is pure, enlightening the eyes. The fear of Yahweh is clean, enduring forever. Yahweh's ordinances are true and righteous altogether.

Psalm 19:7–9 (WEB)

This is the message which we have heard from him and announce to you, that God is light, and in him is no darkness at all. If we say that we have fellowship with him and walk in the darkness, we lie, and don't tell the truth. But if we walk in the light, as he is in the light, we have fellowship with one another, and the blood of Jesus Christ, his Son, cleanses us from all sin. If we say that we have no sin, we deceive ourselves, and the truth is not in us. If we confess our sins, he is faithful and righteous to forgive us the sins, and to cleanse us from all unrighteousness. If we say that we haven't sinned, we make him a liar, and his word is not in us.

1 John 1:5-10 (WEB)

JOURNAL

_____

_____

_____

_____

_____

_____

_____

_____

_____

_____

_____

_____

_____

_____

_____

_____

_____

_____

_____

_____

_____

_____

_____

_____

_____

DAY 6

Lord, give _____ a firm desire to keep your ways. Open his eyes to the consequences and sadness that comes from not following you. Help him to see the purity of your ways so that he would not be guilty of turning from you. In the morning may he seek your decrees and in the night lead him towards your laws. Keep him from sin that he would be blameless and clean before you. Reward him according to his righteousness and show yourself faithful to him as he is faithful to you. Show yourself pure as he is pure. As he reads the scriptures, may he interpret them to be right. May your word bring joy to his heart. Enlighten him through your commandments and truth.

For I have kept Yahweh's ways, and have not wickedly departed from my God. For all his ordinances were before me. As for his statutes, I did not depart from them. I was also perfect toward him. I kept myself from my iniquity. Therefore Yahweh has rewarded me according to my righteousness, According to my cleanness in his eyesight. With the merciful you will show yourself merciful. With the perfect man you will show yourself perfect. With the pure you will show yourself pure. With the crooked you will show yourself shrewd.

2 Samuel 22:22–27 (WEB)

Yahweh's precepts are right, rejoicing the heart. Yahweh's commandment is pure, enlightening the eyes.

Psalm 19:8 (WEB)

JOURNAL

_____

_____

_____

_____

_____

_____

_____

_____

_____

_____

_____

_____

_____

_____

_____

_____

_____

_____

_____

_____

_____

_____

POWER IN OBEDIENCE

...Has Yahweh as great delight in burnt offerings and sacrifices, as in obeying Yahweh's voice? Behold, to obey is better than sacrifice, and to listen than the fat of rams.

Samuel 15:22 (WEB)

Because He Said So

When red letters appear on the page we can't help but to pay closer attention to the scripture. Something about knowing that Jesus said the words snaps us back to attention. We read expectantly knowing that his words will be insightful and life changing but sometimes our excitement dwindles as we read his words. This is especially true in the following passage.

> Jesus answered him, "If a man loves me, he will keep my word. My Father will love him, and we will come to him, and make our home with him. He who doesn't love me doesn't keep my words. The word which you hear isn't mine, but the Father's who sent me.
>
> John 14:23-24 (web)

In the case of John 14, our bubble of expectation is busted because Jesus in so many words says "Do what my Father says."

Nobody wants to hear that. Does anyone wake up saying, "I want to do what someone tells me to do today." Absolutely not. We want to chart our own course, make our decisions, and stretch our free will to the limits.

To make matters worse, Jesus tacks on that only those who *really* love God will do what He says. Have you ever met a Christian who says they don't love God? Christians are eager to admit that they love God but how many times have you met "lovers" of God who are not obedient to God's word? Jesus says that you can't do both. A disobedient Christian is an oxymoron. Ouch.

This scripture gives three blessings for the obedient Christian.

1. The Father will love them.
2. God is with them.
3. God will live within them.

Instead of thinking of consequences of the disobedient, mediate on the blessings of the obedient and ask the Lord to reveal to you ways in which you have been disobedient. Pray for the Holy Spirit's help to give you strength to love God through obedience to his word. Instead of asking God "why?" in those times when he is asking you to be obedient just trust Him. When a child is doing something that will eventually harm them either physically or emotionally, a parent will tell the child to stop doing that thing. Usually, a child (in their own wisdom) will protest and scream "WHY?" Knowing that the child is not mature or wise enough to handle or accept the truth the parent usually responds "Because I said so." Parents usually know best and God always knows best, so be obedient...because he said so.

DAY 7

Father, this morning I lift up _____
to your throne. Ignite him for action in your kingdom
and give him discipline in your ways. Make him sober-
minded and set his hope fully on your grace. Make him
obedient and give him the strength to turn away from
the lusts that easily entangle men of God. Call him to
be holy as you are holy. In obedience to your commands
may he be holy in all he does and says this day. Give him
a love for you that is shown in his obedience towards
your commandments. Empower him to love others as
you have commanded that he would receive his full reward from you. May he always remain in you and obey
your teachings.

Therefore prepare your minds for action, be sober, and set
your hope fully on the grace that will be brought to you at
the revelation of Jesus Christ—as children of obedience, not
conforming yourselves according to your former lusts as in
your ignorance, but just as he who called you is holy, you
yourselves also be holy in all of your behavior; because it is
written, "You shall be holy; for I am holy."

1 Peter 1:13–16 (WEB)

This is love, that we should walk according to his
commandments. This is the commandment, even as you
heard from the beginning, that you should walk in it. For
many deceivers have gone out into the world, those who don't
confess that Jesus Christ came in the flesh. This is the deceiver

and the Antichrist. Watch yourselves, that we don't lose the things which we have accomplished, but that we receive a full reward. Whoever transgresses and doesn't remain in the teaching of Christ, doesn't have God. He who remains in the teaching, the same has both the Father and the Son.

2 John 1:6-9 (WEB)

JOURNAL

_____

_____

_____

_____

_____

_____

_____

_____

_____

_____

_____

_____

_____

_____

_____

_____

_____

_____

_____

_____

_____

_____

_____

_____

_____

_____

_____

DAY 8

Father God, thank you that _____
is not under the law, but under grace. I pray that as a
result of his gratitude for your grace, that he would not
willingly sin in your sight or make excuses and justifica-
tions for his wrongdoing. Knowing that we are slaves to
those whom we obey, I pray that he would be disobedient to the urgings of his flesh. May your righteousness
in him shine more brightly as he is obedient to your
will. If he must be a slave to anything, make him a slave
of righteousness today. Prepare his mind to do anything
that you ask him to do. May his hope be in you as he
acts in ways that may not make sense to others but is in
complete obedience to you. Help him to reject his former ways that were not in obedience to you so that he is
holy in his behavior as well as mind.

What then? Shall we sin, because we are not under law, but
under grace? May it never be! Don't you know that when
you present yourselves as servants and obey someone, you
are the servants of whomever you obey; whether of sin to
death, or of obedience to righteousness? But thanks be to
God, that, whereas you were bondservants of sin, you became
obedient from the heart to that form of teaching to which
you were delivered. Being made free from sin, you became
bondservants of righteousness.

Romans 6:15–18 (WEB)

Therefore prepare your minds for action, be sober, and set your hope fully on the grace that will be brought to you at the revelation of Jesus Christ—as children of obedience, not conforming yourselves according to your former lusts as in your ignorance, but just as he who called you is holy, you yourselves also be holy in all of your behavior;

1 Peter 1:13-15 (WEB)

JOURNAL

DAY 9

Heavenly Father, I pray that _____
truly knows you in the most intimate sense. I pray that
his knowledge and relationship with you would lead
him to be obedient to your commandments. May he
not be a liar, like others around him who say they know
you but do not keep your commandments. May the
truth be in him, may he model his life after the example
of your Son and may your love be perfected within him.
Lord, give him the knowledge that we are not waging
war against people or policies or situations but against
strongholds. Lead him to engage in spiritual warfare by
rebuking everything that goes against the knowledge of
you. May he even make his thoughts obedient to you.

This is how we know that we know him: if we keep his
commandments. One who says, "I know him," and doesn't
keep his commandments, is a liar, and the truth isn't in him.
But whoever keeps his word, God's love has most certainly
been perfected in him. This is how we know that we are in
him: he who says he remains in him ought himself also to
walk just like he walked.

1 John 2:3–6 (WEB)

For though we walk in the flesh, we don't wage war according
to the flesh; for the weapons of our warfare are not of the flesh,
but mighty before God to the throwing down of strongholds,
throwing down imaginations and every high thing that is
exalted against the knowledge of God, and bringing every

thought into captivity to the obedience of Christ; and being in readiness to avenge all disobedience, when your obedience will be made full.

2 Corinthians 10:3-6 (WEB)

JOURNAL

_____

_____

_____

_____

_____

_____

_____

_____

_____

_____

_____

_____

_____

_____

_____

_____

_____

_____

_____

_____

_____

_____

_____

_____

_____

_____

DAY 10

Father God, may _____ abide in your love today. As he is obedient to your commandments, keep him in the fullness of your love. You have commanded that we love one another. I pray that today he would love his enemy as he loves his friends. Give him the willingness to treat others as better than himself. Give him the heart to humbly sacrifice for others as a reflection of your love, for this is what you have commanded. May your spirit purify his soul through his obedience, refresh his spirit through your truth and drive him towards fervent brotherly love.

Even as the Father has loved me, I also have loved you. Remain in my love. If you keep my commandments, you will remain in my love; even as I have kept my Father's commandments, and remain in his love. I have spoken these things to you, that my joy may remain in you, and that your joy may be made full. This is my commandment, that you love one another, even as I have loved you. Greater love has no one than this that someone lay down his life for his friends. You are my friends, if you do whatever I command you.

John 15: 9–14 (web)

Seeing you have purified your souls in your obedience to the truth through the Spirit in sincere brotherly affection, love one another from the heart fervently:

1 Peter 1:22 (web)

JOURNAL

_____
_____
_____
_____
_____
_____
_____
_____
_____
_____
_____
_____
_____
_____
_____
_____
_____
_____
_____
_____
_____
_____

DAY 11

Heavenly Father, give _____ favor and confidence before you this day. Lead him to seek your forgiveness in the specific areas of his life that are not submitted to you. Form sweet desires in his heart as he is obedient to your commandments and give him the boldness to ask you to fulfill these desires. Keep his mind in your truth so that he would believe in the name of your Son above all other names and give him opportunities to love others as he loves himself. May he bring you joy today from his obedience. May your heart be refreshed as he walks in your ways. I pray that he would do even more than you ask of him as a sign of his devotion towards you.

Beloved, if our hearts don't condemn us, we have boldness toward God; and whatever we ask, we receive from him, because we keep his commandments and do the things that are pleasing in his sight. This is his commandment, that we should believe in the name of his Son, Jesus Christ, and love one another, even as he commanded. He who keeps his commandments remains in him, and he in him. By this we know that he remains in us, by the Spirit which he gave us.

1 John 3: 21-24 (WEB)

Yes, brother, let me have joy from you in the Lord. Refresh my heart in the Lord. Having confidence in your obedience, I write to you, knowing that you will do even beyond what I say.

Philemon 1:20-21 (WEB)

JOURNAL

_____
_____
_____
_____
_____
_____
_____
_____
_____
_____
_____
_____
_____
_____
_____
_____
_____
_____
_____
_____
_____
_____
_____
_____
_____

DAY 12

Father, I lift up your son _____
to you this day. Give him a heart for your commandments. May thoughts of murder, adultery, stealing, and
lying not cross his mind. May his hands not be guilty of
breaking your commands. Keep him far from activities
and mind-sets that lead to death. May he honor his family and his relationship with you above all else. Open
his eyes to the people around him who need love and
give him an abundant portion of love to share. May you
see that he listens to your voice, keeps your commands
and delights in your laws. In your grace, bless his family
through his obedience towards you.

He said to him, "Why do you call me good? No one is good
but one, that is, God. But if you want to enter into life, keep
the commandments." He said to him, "Which ones?" Jesus
said, "'You shall not murder.' 'You shall not commit adultery.'
'You shall not steal.' 'You shall not offer false testimony.'
'Honor your father and mother.' And, 'You shall love your
neighbor as yourself.

Matthew 19:17–19 (WEB)

Live in this land, and I will be with you, and will bless you. For
I will give to you, and to your offspring all these lands, and I
will establish the oath which I swore to Abraham your father.
I will multiply your offspring as the stars of the sky, and will
give all these lands to your offspring. In your offspring will all

the nations of the earth be blessed, because Abraham obeyed my voice, and kept my requirements, my commandments, my statutes, and my laws.

Genesis 26: 3-5 (WEB)

JOURNAL

_____

_____

_____

_____

_____

_____

_____

_____

_____

_____

_____

_____

_____

_____

_____

_____

_____

_____

_____

_____

_____

_____

_____

_____

_____

_____

_____

POWER IN WISDOM

For Yahweh gives wisdom.
Out of his mouth comes knowledge
and understanding.

Proverbs 2:6 (WEB)

Godly Wisdom

Solomon loved Yahweh, walking in the statutes of David his father;...In Gibeon, Yahweh appeared to Solomon in a dream by night; and God said, "Ask for what I should give you." Solomon said, "You have shown to your servant David my father great loving kindness, because he walked before you in truth, in righteousness, and in uprightness of heart with you...I am just a little child. I don't know how to go out or come in...Give your servant therefore an understanding heart to judge your people, that I may discern between good and evil; for who is able to judge this great people of yours?" This request pleased the Lord, that Solomon had asked this thing. God said to him, "Because you have asked this thing, and have not asked for yourself long life, nor have you asked for riches for yourself, nor have you asked for the life of your enemies, but have asked for yourself understanding to discern justice; behold, I have done according to your word. Behold, I have given you a wise and understanding heart; so that there has been no one like you before you, and after you none will arise like you.

1 Kings 3:3, 5-6a, 7, 9-12 (web)

When Solomon is mentioned in church circles two things come to mind: The ladies man and the wise man. How he could be both is still a mystery, but we cannot deny the portion of wisdom that God granted him.

If we look at the story closely, it seems that Solomon displayed a measure of wisdom before God granted it to him. He was wise enough to follow the ways of the Lord and discerning enough to ask the right blessing from God. God was thrilled to say "Yes" to this request.

If we are seeking wisdom for a significant situation we must first look to see what small areas God has asked us to be wise in. In this passage, wisdom is described as understanding and discernment.

Would "wise" be an appropriate word to describe the men in your life? Not just the older men but the younger ones as well. Solomon was young when he prayed this prayer and it shows that young men are fully capable of showing wisdom. Here is the message that wisdom has for the men in our lives:

> "To you men, I call!
> I send my voice to the sons of mankind.
> You simple, understand prudence.
> You fools, be of an understanding heart.
> Hear, for I will speak excellent things.
> The opening of my lips is for right things.
> For my mouth speaks truth.
> Wickedness is an abomination to my lips.
> All the words of my mouth are in righteousness.
> There is nothing crooked or perverse in them.
> They are all plain to him who understands,
> right to those who find knowledge.
>
> ~Wisdom (Proverbs 8:4-9)

Be encouraged to read this whole passage in proverbs to get the full message from wisdom and pray with confidence this week knowing that the Lord delights in granting us wisdom.

DAY 13

Father in heaven, I come to you again with
_____ on my heart. I pray that he
would have a holy fear of you. I pray that you would
give him a reverent demeanor towards you. Without
fear of you, there is no wisdom, so I pray that you would
invoke a fear in him that leads to godly wisdom. Bless
him with an understanding of your word so that he
would be effective in leading others to you. As he thinks
on all he encounters through the day, may he submit all
thoughts and ideas to you before he acknowledges them
as truth. I pray that his steps are led by your Spirit. Lord,
give him a calm spirit when tempted to be hotheaded,
give him discernment when tempted to be reckless.

The fear of Yahweh is the beginning of wisdom. All those who
do his work have a good understanding. His praise endures
forever!

Psalms 111:10 (WEB)

A simple man believes everything, but the prudent man
carefully considers his ways. A wise man fears, and shuns evil,
but the fool is hot headed and reckless.

Proverbs 14:15-16 (WEB)

JOURNAL

_____

_____

_____

_____

_____

_____

_____

_____

_____

_____

_____

_____

_____

_____

_____

_____

_____

_____

_____

_____

_____

_____

_____

_____

_____

DAY 14

Father, grant _____ a faith that does not rely on the wisdom of men, but on the power of your Spirit. May he reject the wisdom of this age that leads to death and accept the secret wisdom that can come only from you. Your hidden wisdom was decreed before the ages, and many still do not comprehend it. Reveal to him by your Spirit the beautiful mystery of things unseen and unheard that you have in store for those who you love you. As his faith is tested this week, while he encounters unsuspected trials and as Satan tempts him with worldly wisdom, give him a desire for godly wisdom. Grant your wisdom to him generously when he asks and demolish any seeds of doubt in his mind. Give him a joyful perspective during this time so that he glorifies you and grows in the faith.

We speak wisdom, however, among those who are full grown; yet a wisdom not of this world, nor of the rulers of this world, who are coming to nothing. But we speak God's wisdom in a mystery, the wisdom that has been hidden, which God foreordained before the worlds for our glory, which none of the rulers of this world has known. For had they known it, they wouldn't have crucified the Lord of glory. But as it is written, "Things which an eye didn't see, and an ear didn't hear, which didn't enter into the heart of man, these God has prepared for those who love him." But to us, God revealed them through the Spirit. For the Spirit searches all things, yes, the deep things of God.

1 Corinthians 2:6–10 (WEB)

Count it all joy, my brothers, when you fall into various temptations, knowing that the testing of your faith produces endurance. Let endurance have its perfect work, that you may be perfect and complete, lacking in nothing. But if any of you lacks wisdom, let him ask of God, who gives to all liberally and without reproach; and it will be given to him. But let him ask in faith, without any doubting, for he who doubts is like a wave of the sea, driven by the wind and tossed.

James 1:2-6 (WEB)

JOURNAL

DAY 15

Father, give _____ clean lips today. Bless his lips to utter wisdom and his mouth to speak of righteousness. May he wisely use the power in his tongue to proclaim justice in the midst of injustice. May the words that he speaks today become seeds that bear fruit for your kingdom. Keep a watch over his mouth, so that he would only speak words of life. Lord, humble him to realize today that even his strength is foolishness in your eyes but encourage him with the knowledge that you choose the foolish things of the world to shame the wise in his own eyes. May his wisdom be that he boasts only in you.

The mouth of the righteous talks of wisdom. His tongue speaks justice.

Psalms 37:30 (WEB)

Because the foolishness of God is wiser than men, and the weakness of God is stronger than men. For you see your calling, brothers, that not many are wise according to the flesh, not many mighty, and not many noble; but God chose the foolish things of the world that he might put to shame those who are wise. God chose the weak things of the world, that he might put to shame the things that are strong;

1 Corinthians 1:25-27 (WEB)

JOURNAL

DAY 16

Lord, I pray that you would see the unwavering faith that _____ has in your Son and his love towards your saints and bless him accordingly with the spirit of wisdom and of revelation in the knowledge of you. May he be wise enough to give all praise and thanksgiving to you. Give him a daily desire to come before you daily on his knees to seek your wisdom. If there be any area of his life that does not reverence you, bring it to his minds, convict his hearts to repent and grant them a holy fear of you. Shine a light on the evil in his life and drive him to depart from it.

For this cause I also, having heard of the faith in the Lord Jesus which is among you, and the love which you have toward all the saints, don't cease to give thanks for you, making mention of you in my prayers, that the God of our Lord Jesus Christ, the Father of glory, may give to you a spirit of wisdom and revelation in the knowledge of him.

Ephesians 1:15–17 (web)

"To man he said, 'Behold, the fear of the Lord,that is wisdom. To depart from evil is understanding."

Job 28:28 (web)

JOURNAL

_____

_____

_____

_____

_____

_____

_____

_____

_____

_____

_____

_____

_____

_____

_____

_____

_____

_____

_____

_____

_____

_____

_____

_____

_____

DAY 17

Dear God, your word says that those who find wisdom are blessed, so today I pray that _____ would search for wisdom as if he is searching for a misplaced stack of $100 bills. I pray that you would bless his search and grant him with a powerful wisdom that comes only from above. Help him to experience wisdom in such a way that he values it more than anything on this earth. Grant him a wisdom that leads to peace, long life, spiritual riches, and honor. Lord, speak to his heart about the wisdom that he has despised. Speak to him in such a way that he cannot doubt that he has heard from you. Lord, show him the people in his life whose wisdom is foolishness and give him the strength to separate himself. Remind him of the lessons he learned from his father and mother, godly mentors and pastors.

Happy is the man who finds wisdom, the man who gets understanding. For her good profit is better than getting silver, and her return is better than fine gold. She is more precious than rubies. None of the things you can desire are to be compared to her. Length of days is in her right hand. In her left hand are riches and honor. Her ways are ways of pleasantness. All her paths are peace.

Proverbs 3:13–17 (web)

The proverbs of Solomon, the son of David, king of Israel to know wisdom and instruction; to discern the words of understanding; to receive instruction in wise dealing, in righteousness, justice, and equity; to give prudence to the simple, knowledge and discretion to the young man: that the wise man may hear, and increase in learning: that the man of understanding may attain to sound counsel: to understand a proverb, and parables, the words and riddles of the wise. The fear of Yahweh is the beginning of knowledge; but the foolish despise wisdom and instruction.

My son, listen to your father's instruction, and don't forsake your mother's teaching:

Proverbs 1:1-8 (WEB)

JOURNAL

_____

_____

_____

_____

_____

_____

_____

_____

_____

_____

_____

_____

_____

_____

_____

_____

_____

_____

_____

_____

_____

_____

_____

_____

_____

_____

_____

_____

_____

DAY 18

Dear Father, make _____ wise and understanding among his friends, family and enemies. Let his actions demonstrate the humility in wisdom. Free his heart of any bitterness, jealousy, self-ambition, and pride. Open him to see that these things are truly demonic and cause him to turn from them. Give him a wisdom that is pure, peaceable, gentle, full of mercy, good fruits, impartial, and sincere. Lord, show him the areas in his life where he considers himself wise. Reveal to him the areas of his life where he has decided that his ways are better than yours and his thoughts are more relevant than your thoughts. Give him a spirit of repentance towards his own wisdom and may he shun evil within himself. Urge him to trust in your ways alone and remind him to honor you with all that you have given him.

Who is wise and understanding among you? Let him show by his good conduct that his deeds are done in gentleness of wisdom. But if you have bitter jealousy and selfish ambition in your heart, don't boast and don't lie against the truth. This wisdom is not that which comes down from above, but is earthly, sensual, and demonic. For where jealousy and selfish ambition are, there is confusion and every evil deed. But the wisdom that is from above is first pure, then peaceful, gentle, reasonable, full of mercy and good fruits, without partiality, and without hypocrisy. Now the fruit of righteousness is sown in peace by those who make peace.

James 3:13–18 (WEB)

Trust in Yahweh with all your heart, and don't lean on your own understanding. In all your ways acknowledge him, and he will make your paths straight. Don't be wise in your own eyes. Fear Yahweh, and depart from evil. It will be health to your body, and nourishment to your bones. Honor Yahweh with your substance, with the first fruits of all your increase:

Proverbs 3:5-9 (WEB)

JOURNAL

_____

_____

_____

_____

_____

_____

_____

_____

_____

_____

_____

_____

_____

_____

_____

_____

_____

_____

_____

_____

_____

_____

_____

POWER IN EXHORTATION

Beware, brothers, lest perhaps there be in any one of you an evil heart of unbelief, in falling away from the living God; but exhort one another day by day, so long as it is called "today"; lest anyone of you be hardened by the deceitfulness of sin.

Hebrews 3:12–13 (WEB)

Speak the Truth in Love

Exhortation is not only a spiritual gift but a responsibility of all children of God to a certain degree. While one may not have the gift of exhorting large crowds, we all have the ability to exhort one person at a time as God brings people into our lives.

Exhortation is:

> "...the special ability to counsel or challenge others toward a healthy relationship with Jesus Christ. Often, the gift of Exhortation is utilized to motivate the Church in general or a Christ Follower in particular, to make God-honoring choices...The gift of Exhortation is somewhat similar to the role of the Old Testament prophets in challenging God's people to remain faithful. While the prophets were not immediately valued, and often persecuted, their service was indispensable to the spiritual health and vitality of the biblical faith community...People with the gift of Exhortation feel a deep responsibility before God to challenge and encourage those that may be taking a path that does not honor the Lord, to correct their misguided choices."[5]

We have many examples of exhortation in the Old and New Testament. These people of God were not always the most popular and said the hard things that people did not want to hear, yet, the kingdom of God was fulfilled because of the truth they shared.

Moses, Joshua, Paul, Barnabas and many more were exhorters. Note the exhortation of Moses below to the Israelites:

> It shall be, when Yahweh your God brings you into the land which he swore to your fathers, to Abraham, to Isaac, and to Jacob, to give you, great and goodly cities, which you didn't build, and houses full of all good things, which you didn't fill, and cisterns dug out, which you didn't dig, vineyards and olive trees, which you didn't plant, and you shall eat and be full; then beware lest you forget Yahweh, who brought you out of the land of Egypt, out of the house of bondage. You shall fear Yahweh your God; and you shall serve him, and shall swear by his name. You shall not go after other gods, of the gods of the peoples who are around you;for Yahweh your God among you is a jealous God; lest the anger of Yahweh your God be kindled against you, and he destroy you from off the face of the earth.
>
> Deuteronomy 6:10-15 (WEB)

Let us pray that the men in our lives would have the same boldness, passion, truth and grace as the saints to exhort their families and brothers and sisters in the faith.

DAY 19

Thank you, Heavenly Father, for the gifts you have given to _____. I pray that the gift of exhortation would be given to him according to your grace. Help him to encourage the body of Christ by gently teaching people to serve through their gifts by example. May he never be lacking in zeal and spiritual fervor. May his mouth continually speak truth to build up his brothers and sisters in Christ. Lord, as he exhorts others inspire him to live the life that he encourages others to live. Challenge him to set a higher standard for himself than those around him. Calm his temper so that he is not easily angered and give him humility so that he puts others above himself. Make him a faithful lover of your word, full of self-control and holiness.

Having gifts differing according to the grace that was given to us, if prophecy, let us prophesy according to the proportion of our faith; or service, let us give ourselves to service; or he who teaches, to his teaching; or he who exhorts, to his exhorting: he who gives, let him do it with liberality; he who rules, with diligence; he who shows mercy, with cheerfulness.

Romans 12:6–8 (WEB)

For the overseer must be blameless, as God's steward; not self-pleasing, not easily angered, not given to wine, not violent, not greedy for dishonest gain; but given to hospitality, a lover of good, sober minded, fair, holy, self-controlled; holding to the faithful word which is according to the teaching, that he may be able to exhort in the sound doctrine, and to convict those who contradict him.

Titus 1:7-9 (WEB)

JOURNAL

_____

_____

_____

_____

_____

_____

_____

_____

_____

_____

_____

_____

_____

_____

_____

_____

_____

_____

_____

_____

_____

_____

_____

_____

_____

DAY 20

Father God, I lift up _____ to you today. Grant him the desire to lead others to you with not only his actions but his words. Give him a boldness to tell others the truth of the gospel and how to experience your salvation and forgiveness of sins. May he bear witness with his words by speaking firm truth to his family and those in his circle of influence. Through his exhortation, may many be added to your kingdom. I pray that he would always be ready to give a word of testimony and truth when called upon and that others would believe from hearing his faith.

Peter said to them, "Repent, and be baptized, every one of you, in the name of Jesus Christ for the forgiveness of sins, and you will receive the gift of the Holy Spirit. For the promise is to you, and to your children, and to all who are far off, even as many as the Lord our God will call to himself." With many other words he testified, and exhorted them, saying, "Save yourselves from this crooked generation!" Then those who gladly received his word were baptized. There were added that day about three thousand souls.

Acts 2:38–41 (WEB)

After the reading of the law and the prophets, the rulers of the synagogue sent to them, saying, "Brothers, if you have any word of exhortation for the people, speak." Paul stood up, and beckoning with his hand said, "Men of Israel, and you who fear God, listen.

Acts 13:15-16 (WEB)

JOURNAL

_____

_____

_____

_____

_____

_____

_____

_____

_____

_____

_____

_____

_____

_____

_____

_____

_____

_____

_____

_____

_____

_____

_____

_____

_____

_____

DAY 21

Dear Father, with the power of your Spirit, I charge _____ to be ready to preach your word in and out of season, to patiently reprove, rebuke, and exhort. Give him a sharp mind to recognize false doctrines and teachings that only appeal to the passions of the masses. May his words, inspired by you, turn people away from listening to lies and philosophies that have originated from Satan. May your Spirit lead him to be fruitful in the ministry of evangelism. Lord, as he opens his mouth to exhort let it be out of an undivided and clean heart. Let him speak only truth that comes from you so that you can entrust him with continual words of knowledge from you. May he seek only to please you in his words and not man or church or leaders. Test his heart Lord before he opens his mouth.

I command you therefore before God and the Lord Jesus Christ, who will judge the living and the dead at his appearing and his Kingdom: preach the word; be urgent in season and out of season; reprove, rebuke, and exhort, with all patience and teaching. For the time will come when they will not listen to the sound doctrine, but, having itching ears, will heap up for themselves teachers after their own lusts; and will turn away their ears from the truth, and turn aside to fables. But you be sober in all things, suffer hardship, do the work of an evangelist, and fulfill your ministry.

2 Timothy 4:1-5 (WEB)

For our exhortation is not of error, nor of uncleanness, nor in deception. But even as we have been approved by God to be entrusted with the Good News, so we speak; not as pleasing men, but God, who tests our hearts.

1 Thessalonians 2:3-4 (WEB)

JOURNAL

_____

_____

_____

_____

_____

_____

_____

_____

_____

_____

_____

_____

_____

_____

_____

_____

_____

_____

_____

_____

_____

_____

_____

DAY 22

Father God, as you used the exhortations of John the Baptist to point to you, I pray that you would use the exhortations of _____ to bring You glory. As he opens his mouth to exhort, I pray that others would no longer see him, but see you and be drawn to you in an unmistakable way. May he never apologize for speaking freely of your justice and judgment and may he often speak of your enduring love. Help him to naturally encourage others to continue in the faith when they are going through trials. Give him gentleness and boldness to speak truth to those who are being afflicted so that they would never lose their faith.

John answered them all, "I indeed baptize you with water, but he comes who is mightier than I, the strap of whose sandals I am not worthy to loosen. He will baptize you in the Holy Spirit and fire, whose fan is in his hand, and he will thoroughly cleanse his threshing floor, and will gather the wheat into his barn; but he will burn up the chaff with unquenchable fire. Then with many other exhortations he preached good news to the people.

Luke 3:16–18 (WEB)

...confirming the souls of the disciples, exhorting them to continue in the faith, and that through many afflictions we must enter into God's Kingdom.

Acts 14:22(WEB)

JOURNAL

DAY 23

Heavenly Father, I pray that others would be a witness to how _____ is genuinely laboring to proclaim the gospel of truth so that they would be inspired to do the same. Make his words and conduct holy and blameless in your sight so that his witness is not tarnished. Make him like a spiritual father to those you entrust him with, fill his mouth with encouragement as he charges others to remain on the path of holiness. Lord, give him an assertive spirit to rebuke those who need it and a sweet spirit to encourage those who are weary. Make him patient towards all so that others would you see your character within him.

For you remember, brothers, our labor and travail; for working night and day, that we might not burden any of you, we preached to you the Good News of God. You are witnesses with God, how holy, righteously, and blamelessly we behaved ourselves toward you who believe. As you know, we exhorted, comforted, and implored every one of you, as a father does his own children, to the end that you should walk worthily of God, who calls you into his own Kingdom and glory.

1 Thessalonians 2:9–12 (WEB)

We exhort you, brothers, admonish the disorderly, encourage the faint-hearted, support the weak, be patient toward all. See that no one returns evil for evil to anyone, but always follow after that which is good, for one another, and for all.

1 Thessalonians 5: 14-15 (WEB)

JOURNAL

DAY 24

Father, open _____ mouth to prophesy your undeniable truths today. May his words be used to build up your people and bring about your kingdom on earth. Send those with weary hearts his way that he may encourage them and set those with hurting hearts on his path, that he may console them in your name. May his words point to heaven today and may you the open ears of those around him to hear your truth. Soften his heart to endure all words of exhortation that he himself has received through your word, spiritual leaders and brothers in Christ. May he complete every good work that brings about your will.

Follow after love, and earnestly desire spiritual gifts, but especially that you may prophesy. For he who speaks in another language speaks not to men, but to God; for no one understands; but in the Spirit he speaks mysteries. But he who prophesies speaks to men for their edification, exhortation, and consolation.

1 Corinthians 14:1–3 (WEB)

Now may the God of peace, who brought again from the dead the great shepherd of the sheep with the blood of an eternal covenant, our Lord Jesus, make you complete in every good work to do his will, working in you that which is well pleasing in his sight, through Jesus Christ, to whom be the glory forever and ever. Amen. But I exhort you, brothers, endure the word of exhortation, for I have written to you in few words.

Hebrews 13:20-22 (WEB)

JOURNAL

POWER IN RESPONSIBILITY

He has shown you, O man, what is
good. What does Yahweh require of
you, but to act justly, to love mercy,
and to walk humbly with your God?

Micah 6:8 (WEB)

Head of the Household

"But if anyone doesn't provide for his own, and especially his own household, he has denied the faith, and is worse than an unbeliever."

1 Timothy 5:8 (WEB)

There is an unfortunate trend of women heading their households in the United States. This trend is not just true of poor or minority groups, but is common among all races and socioeconomic groups. This trend is strongly correlated with women who have children outside of marriage.

About 4 out of 10 children were born to unwed mothers. Of all single-parent families in the U.S., single mothers make up the majority. According to the U.S. Census Bureau, **Out of 12.2 million single parent families in 2012, more than 80% were headed by single mothers**. Today, 1 in 3 children—a total of 15 million—are being raised without a father. Of that group, nearly half live below the poverty line.—U.S. Census Bureau—Table FG10. Family Groups: 2012

Many children may be growing up with the mindset that men are generally irresponsible due to the large number of single mothers. Even in some two parent homes, I have heard women say that they feel they are a single parent. God intended for men to be heads of the household but many men are failing to reach their God given potential to lead responsibly.

God calls all of his children to lead responsible lives. The grace of God should inspire his people to be more responsible with all that they are given. Accepting men as head of the household is difficult for women who live with men who are not responsible to God's call to lead. But instead of bashing men and complaining about how they are never around when you need them and how they are not spiritually mature let use our energies to pray this week. Pray that they would live out their full potential as heads of our households by leading responsibly.

DAY 25

Heavenly Father, you have given your children responsibility and I pray that _____ would understand his responsibility as a man of God. May he be seated firmly in you, unwavering and immovable and never tire of doing the works of your hands. May he always be confident that you will bless the humble works of his hands. As he is consistently responsible in the small things, show him victory in the larger things. Lord, show him his spiritual responsibility to gently restore others who are in error and keep him strong so that he does not fall into the same error. Remind him of the privilege he has to fulfill the law of Christ by bearing the burdens of others. Daily remind him of his responsibility to share what your spirit teaches him to others. Remind him that he is responsible for all he reaps based on what he has sown emotionally, spiritually, financially and spiritually.

The sting of death is sin, and the power of sin is the law. But thanks be to God, who gives us the victory through our Lord Jesus Christ. Therefore, my beloved brothers, be steadfast, immovable, always abounding in the Lord's work, because you know that your labor is not in vain in the Lord.

1 Corinthians 15:56–58(WEB)

Brothers, even if a man is caught in some fault, you who are spiritual must restore such a one in a spirit of gentleness;

looking to yourself so that you also aren't tempted. Bear one another's burdens, and so fulfill the law of Christ. For if a man thinks himself to be something when he is nothing, he deceives himself. But let each man test his own work, and then he will take pride in himself and not in his neighbor. For each man will bear his own burden. But let him who is taught in the word share all good things with him who teaches. Don't be deceived. God is not mocked, for whatever a man sows, that he will also reap.

Galatians 6:1-7 (WEB)

JOURNAL

_____

_____

_____

_____

_____

_____

_____

_____

_____

_____

_____

_____

_____

_____

_____

_____

_____

_____

_____

_____

_____

_____

_____

_____

DAY 26

Father, remind _____ of his responsibility as a worker. May he never be found to be lazy or taking advantage of his employer. Whatever he does, may he do as if he is working directly for you. May he be submissive to his leaders and overseers in honor of you, knowing that you will reward him at just the right time. As Christ served lowly man, help him to serve all that you place in his path. Lord, as a leader, help him to treat those under his authority with dignity and respect. May he treat them graciously because he knows that you treat him graciously. Reveal to him father that although it is your spirit that saves souls that he still plays a significant part in the kingdom by what he plants and waters. Remind him that he is your fellow worker and that he will be rewarded accordingly.

And whatever you do, work heartily, as for the Lord, and not for men, knowing that from the Lord you will receive the reward of the inheritance; for you serve the Lord Christ. But he who does wrong will receive again for the wrong that he has done, and there is no partiality. Masters, give to your servants that which is just and equal, knowing that you also have a Master in heaven.

Colossians 3:23–4:1 (web)

So then neither he who plants is anything, nor he who waters, but God who gives the increase. Now he who plants and he who waters are the same, but each will receive his own reward according to his own labor. For we are God's fellow workers. You are God's farming, God's building.

1 Corinthians 3:7-9 (WEB)

JOURNAL

_____

_____

_____

_____

_____

_____

_____

_____

_____

_____

_____

_____

_____

_____

_____

_____

_____

_____

_____

_____

_____

_____

DAY 27

Heavenly Father, remind _____ today that you have made him responsible to care for your children. Open his heart to share meals with the hungry and give him a generous heart to delegate your finances to those in need. Give him a desire to treat strangers like friends and provide comforts for the poor. Give him a caring heart so that he would be mindful enough to visit those in the hospital, write letters to those in prison and spend time with the lonely. Help him to see his life as a gift from you and therefore be honored to daily serve you. Teach him to know your will and obey it. May he prepare himself and his family for your coming. As you increase his earthly blessings and responsibilities, remind him that much will be required of him.

For I was hungry, and you gave me food to eat. I was thirsty, and you gave me drink. I was a stranger, and you took me in. I was naked, and you clothed me. I was sick, and you visited me. I was in prison, and you came to me.

Matthew 25:35–36 (WEB)

But if that servant says in his heart, 'My lord delays his coming,' and begins to beat the menservants and the maidservants, and to eat and drink, and to be drunken, then the lord of that servant will come in a day when he isn't expecting him, and in an hour that he doesn't know, and will cut him in two, and place his portion with the unfaithful. That servant, who knew his lord's will, and didn't prepare, nor do what he wanted, will be beaten with many stripes, but he who didn't know, and did things worthy of stripes, will be beaten with few stripes. To whomever much is given, of him will much be required; and to whom much was entrusted, of him more will be asked.

Luke 12:45-48 (WEB)

JOURNAL

_____

_____

_____

_____

_____

_____

_____

_____

_____

_____

_____

_____

_____

_____

_____

_____

_____

_____

_____

_____

_____

_____

_____

_____

_____

_____

DAY 28

Father God, remind _____ today that he was created to be the head in his household. Make him a leader not just in word, but in his sacrificial actions. Let love lead his decisions and not selfishness. Fill his heart with a love rooted in Christ for himself and for the woman you have entrusted to him. Make him holy and without blemish so that he would be presented spotless and in splendor before you. May he increase all that you have made him a steward of. May he show you this he is responsible and faithful enough to receive more from you. Reveal to him the areas of his life where he has not shown himself responsible.

For the husband is the head of the wife, and Christ also is the head of the assembly, being himself the savior of the body. But as the assembly is subject to Christ, so let the wives also be to their own husbands in everything. Husbands, love your wives, even as Christ also loved the assembly, and gave himself up for it; that he might sanctify it, having cleansed it by the washing of water with the word, that he might present the assembly to himself gloriously, not having spot or wrinkle or any such thing; but that it should be holy and without defect. Even so husbands also ought to love their own wives as their own bodies. He who loves his own wife loves himself.

Ephesians 5:23–28 (WEB)

'For I tell you that to everyone who has, will more be given; but from him who doesn't have, even that which he has will be taken away from him.

Luke 19:26 (WEB)

Nina Elaine Borum

JOURNAL

_____

_____

_____

_____

_____

_____

_____

_____

_____

_____

_____

_____

_____

_____

_____

_____

_____

_____

_____

_____

_____

_____

DAY 29

Father God, lay on _____ heart and mind today his duty and responsibility to go out from his comfort zone and disciple others in your name. May he lead others to be baptized by your Spirit and in your Son's name. Gift him with the ability to teach others the heart behind your commandments and be with him as he faithfully lives out your call. Lord, I rebuke the spirit of blame in his life. If there be any situations that he has decided to blame others for, convict him. If there be any actions that he has made excuses for, humble him quickly. Teach him to take responsibility for his actions.

Go, and make disciples of all nations, baptizing them in the name of the Father and of the Son and of the Holy Spirit, teaching them to observe all things that I commanded you. Behold, I am with you always, even to the end of the age. Amen.

Matthew 28: 19–20 (WEB)

The man said, "The woman whom you gave to be with me, she gave me fruit from the tree, and I ate it."

Genesis 3:12 (WEB)

JOURNAL

DAY 30

Heavenly Father, I appeal to you on behalf of
_____. I pray that he would will-
ingly present his life to you as a holy sacrifice. Give him
the desire to take the small and seemingly insignificant
things in his daily life and lay them at your altar. May he
never blend in so much with the world that he does not
look like he is a part of your family. Remind him that he
is to be a light in the darkness and the salt of the earth.
Lord, help him to consider all his ways and work as if
he is working for you in all things. I rebuke the sluggard
spirit in any area of his life.

Therefore I urge you, brothers, by the mercies of God, to
present your bodies a living sacrifice, holy, acceptable to God,
which is your spiritual service. Don't be conformed to this
world, but be transformed by the renewing of your mind,
so that you may prove what is the good, well-pleasing, and
perfect will of God.

Romans 12: 1–2 (WEB)

Go to the ant, you sluggard. Consider her ways, and be wise;

Proverbs 6:6 (WEB)

JOURNAL

Note to the Prayer Warrior

I hope that you did not read through this book. It was written for you to pray through! Just because the thirty days is over does not mean that the battle is. The enemy is just waiting to pounce as soon as you take a break from spiritual warfare. Put your armor back on and fight for truth in the lives of the men you love.

I wrote the poem below one morning as I was preparing to pray. May it be an encouragement and inspiration to you.

Fighting with you,
Nina

Warrior Princess

Moonlight

Before the day breaks
I rise to my feet
To prepare for the hellish
Chaos that is planned for me.
Moving to the beat of Your heart
I sway in victory

Because you have already
Granted it to me.
Like a chereokee tribe dancing
Before their enemies defeat.
I dance to the Spirit's heart beat.

Midnight

My flesh is weak from fasting
And my spirit man is strong
Disrobing the garments of this world
I bathe in spiritual songs.
Cleansing myself before
I put the battle armor on.
The prince of the world
Has viciously ruled the night
But at the first sight of light
I will be the first to strike
My soul is ready to fight.

Twilight

The belt of truth around my waist
Protecting my heart is the breastplate
The sandals that bring forth peace
The offensive sword that protects me
Not forgetting the helmet of salvation that delivers me.
I go boldly before the heavenly throne
Calling on the name who holds my soul
I receive the anointing of the righteous one
My words speak life as I pray in the spirit
Binding and loosing on earth what is in heaven.
The angels gather round me
To receive orders for battle

For God has given me dominion
And authority.
At the sound of my voice
Chains will be broken and demons will flee.
For the Lord of universe
Favors me.

Sunrise

Father, Son and Spirit
The trinity shines through me
I have no fear of this day
I walk victoriously.
My battle scars do not compare
To the wounds I've inflicted
Upon the ancient enemy.
I'm a warrior princess
Hell doesn't mess with me.

Bonus Prayers

PURITY

In the power of Jesus's name, I claim purity to be released in _____ life. I command purity to penetrate the impure places in his heart, mind, soul, and body. I thank you because I know that the light of purity is shedding light in the darkest places of his life. I command the impurity to flee from his spirit now. By faith, I believe these things to be done.

OBEDIENCE

In the power of Jesus' name, I claim obedience to be released in _____ life. I bind the spirit of disobedience from his life this day. I take authority over the spirits of distrust, rebellion, and self-will that seek to ruin his life and bind them. They have no place in his life. I loose unwavering trust and humble submission into his life day. By faith, I believe these things to be done.

WISDOM

In the power of Jesus's name, I command wisdom to be released in _____ life. I take authority over the spirit of folly and worldly wisdom and bind it in the name of Jesus. I loose the gift of discernment into his life, that he would know your works from the works of Satan. Bless your servant with a heart of understanding and give wisdom generously to him. I rebuke all doubt that would hinder your gift of wisdom, for we know that wisdom is only granted when asked in faith and without doubt. By faith, I believe these things to be done.

EXHORTATION

In the power of Jesus's name, I command the gift of exhortation to be released in _____ life. Open wide his mouth to boldly speak forth truth to anyone that crosses his path whose heart is ready to receive the truth. I take authority over the spirit of laziness that would keep him from studying your word; and therefore keep from sharing biblical words of knowledge and encouragement. I renounce the spirit of fear that would keep him from speaking truth in times where the truth is unpopular. By faith, I believe these things to be done.

RESPONSIBILITY

In the power of Jesus's name, I command a generous portion of responsibility to be released in _____ life. May he always be aware that you have first and foremost called him to be holy and sanctified. I bind the attitude of carelessness that would keep him from taking up his responsibility to live out your call. I cast down the strongholds of sexual immorality in his life because you have said that he is responsible for his body which is your temple and is to be honored in all things. Your holy call is irrevocable and therefore he is responsible to live it out. May he proudly take up his responsibility to do justice, love mercy, and walk humbly with you.

Endnotes

1. E.M. Bounds 1985. Power Through Prayer (7)
2. Gesenius, W., & Tregelles, S. P. (2003). *Gesenius' Hebrew and Chaldee lexicon to the Old Testament Scriptures* (676). Bellingham, WA: Logos Bible Software.
3. Louw, J. P., & Nida, E. A. (1996). *Vol. 1*: *Greek-English lexicon of the New Testament: Based on semantic domains* (electronic ed. of the 2nd edition.) (408). New York: United Bible Societies.
4. Duncan-Williams, Nicholas (2012-03-29). The Incredible Powers of a Praying Woman (Kindle Locations 153-163). Kindle Edition.
5. "Exhortation." Access Me. E-Church Essentials LLC 2013.

www.ingramcontent.com/pod-product-compliance
Lightning Source LLC
La Vergne TN
LVHW051413080426
835508LV00022B/3072